Pastorals

PETER MCDONALD was born and grew up in Belfast. He won the Newdigate Prize for poetry and an Eric Gregory award. He has taught at the universities of Cambridge and Bristol, and has been Christopher Tower Student and Tutor in Poetry at Christ Church, Oxford since 1999. A prominent critic of modern and contemporary poetry, he has published a book on Louis MacNeice, a study of Northern Irish poetry and, most recently, *Serious Poetry: Form and Authority from Yeats to Hill* (OUP, 2002). He has edited MacNeice's *Selected Plays*, and is also the editor of his forthcoming *Collected Poems*.

Also by Peter McDonald

Poetry
Biting the Wax
Adam's Dream

Criticism
Louis MacNeice: The Poet in his Contexts
Mistaken Identities: Poetry and Northern Ireland
Serious Poetry: Form and Authority from Yeats to Hill

PETER McDONALD

Pastorals

CARCANET

First published in Great Britain in 2004 by
Carcanet Press Limited
Alliance House
Cross Street
Manchester M2 7AQ
Copyright © Peter McDonald 2004
The right of Peter McDonald to be identified as the author of this work has
been asserted by him in accordance with the Copyright, Designs and Patents Act
of 1988
A CIP catalogue record for this book is available from the British Library
ISBN 1 85754 752 7
The publisher acknowledges financial assistance from Arts Council England

Typeset in Bembo by XL Publishing Services, Tiverton
Printed and bound in England by SRP Ltd, Exeter

in memory of Duncan McDonald
1921–2002

Ποιμενίαν ἄγλωσσος ἀν᾿ ὀργάδα μέλπεται Ἀχὼ
ἀντίθρουν πτανοῖς ὑστερόφωνον ὄπα.

An echo is when sound comes back late, and misses itself,
with no tongue to call its own: in deep pasture-land
birdsong is repeating when the birds themselves have flown
out of earshot — have flown straight into the daylight
of broad fields, echoless, where voices get lost on the wind.

Contents

Two Trees

Weeds upon weeds, sticky with cables and jags,
made the path I was on hardly a path at all,
more a net of stalks and shoots, zig-zags
slowing my pace right down to a crawl
as I picked my way, if way you could call
it, half that morning in a drenched glare
after the hound, and its nose-down, long-haul
trek on some urgent but obscure affair
still far from over, and in which I had some share.

Blue dragonflies were switched on by the sun
and clattered into action; warily
I cleared the obstacles one by one,
but knew I was lost; all eyes were on me
(I didn't doubt for a moment they would see),
and what had felt like silence an hour ago
had turned now to a full cacophony
of things conferring, scuttling, in the know:
an audience perhaps, intent on this one show.

I came to a cleared hollow, where two trees
stood off from one another, bright with moss
that covered them like fur or a disease;
some rain was falling now, while just across
from where the trees put on a greenish gloss
as water caught in drops on their long hair,
I saw myself waiting and at a loss
for where to go, or whether I should dare
the wrong way out; the hound was neither here nor there.

So I stayed alone, at the far end of my luck,
searching the daylight for a way to go,
the path to one side, on the other the stuck
souls of Fraelissa and Fradubio
confirmed in bark and moss, always to grow
apart in separately wordless pain,
able only to move in the wind, with no
eyes to cry out, and just the good rain
for tears, not once to touch each other ever again.

The Cup

All around the lip, twisting and winding, tendrils of ivy
have stretched over themselves, with clusters of yellow berries
picked out hard and minute in the sculpted wood.
A girl is leaning underneath; she is not of this world
by the look of her, one hand holding the hem of her dress,
the other toying with a gemstone between her breasts,

while on either side of her, two big men stand glaring
at each other, having their say with faces full of bile,
and taking turns with dirty looks and bitter words
to which she is all but oblivious; she smiles slightly
as she looks at the one, then she looks at the other smiling,
while they go at it hammer and tongs, both in love with her:
the sad truth shows in their sore and haunted eyes.

Next to these, you can see an old codger perched on a rock,
a fisherman with his net, stripped here to the waist,
and ready to make a cast far out over the water
so that he seems to balance back and aim with all his strength
like a man half his age; on his neck the veins and sinews
are drawing tight as he concentrates, steadies himself,
and remembers only his body, which is no longer old.

Beside him, far away, is a boy who couldn't care less,
watching (*not* watching, in fact) the vineyard terraces
near harvest-time; as he drapes himself over a wall of stones
a pair of foxes get down to work, one making light
of his breakfast, the other snatching bunch after bunch of grapes,
and all this time the little guy works and works, taken up
entirely with a fragile, half-finished wicker cage
he'll use as a trap for crickets, and their prison,
plaiting and turning the stalks, snapping them, starting again.

Below this, pointy acanthus gathers and multiplies,
and the base of the cup is leaves, then leaves upon leaves.

Theocritus

10

A Gloss

Running like that, his arm in hers,
two wobbly penstrokes, characters

against a wall in streetlit rain,
they make a word I can't explain

or dare not, as they pelt away
from us, and what we hardly say,

towards some obscure privacy

(for sleep or sorrow, anger, sex?)
maintaining their mysterious checks

and balances, impossibly.

Visitors

The little girl who meets me in the tomb
and asks for *caramela, caramela*,
can hardly make me out, and in no time
when I am gone, she will no longer tell
one boiled sweet from another people give
her in the musty shadows, casting shadows
into this echoing, used-out grave
where every day they gather, and she follows.

As I step out from the dead dark to the sun
I meet a line of uncles, visitors
in hats and coats, their shadows all but gone,
who leave me with my hands full, looking down
the red-tiled hall under high concrete stairs,
and say goodbye with sweeties and half-crowns.

At Castlereagh Church

The sun goes out in pink and purple
late on a late Easter Sunday,
while at the gates a courting couple
begin to take their winding way
from church down towards Gilnahirk,
through whin-blossom and blackcurrant
along the hedgerows where they walk:
primroses, docken and wild mint.

My father in his travelling clothes,
my mother in her summer coat:
they feel the chill, and walk in close
to each other on a dropping road
past fields and gardens, weeks before
the clematis will risk a flower.

Pastoral

Spring this week came breezing in
early, unconsidered, rash,
fighting where it could not win
no-colours of earth and ash

only with the frailest things:
blossom holding itself tight,
crocuses with folded wings
glancing flame, a change in light

switching bare trees into life
morning after morning, though
frost may come yet like a knife
late, and there may be late snow

coming from somewhere even now.
Wakened early, in the dark,
miles from you, I saw a bough
flare with buds, and make its mark

over against the odds; I saw
everything half-edged with fire
when both heart and eyes are raw:
nothing shaped, nothing entire.

You, I know, were late to bed
while I paused to let the day
make good what I might have said
with whatever I might say.

The Scald

Half-way up, on the inside, here,
of my right forearm, is the scald:
a whitish outline like a mended tear
in skin that is thirty years healed
– or more than thirty, as it must be –
and was my wrist, the time I scaled
the kitchen table, when a pot of tea
came down; the burn smacked first, then held

and held on while the heat pressed hard
but where, now, you can touch, and touch again,
where you can push into the soft skin
and put your finger on this pucker-scarred
ragged circle the size, say, of a coin,
then take your lips and touch them to the scald.

Air and Angels

The road might as well be made from sun and water,
the way it has shimmered and glared this half-hour
as it snakes along from here to there;
and it would lead you on, if you'd a mind
to go – three parts mirage, something
and nothing, light for the sunblind –
until I lost you in the flash and flare
with everything close, but miles off; tricks and lies
in what you see: all hit and miss,
for a cloud comes, as it will, and
the light changes anyway in a second
to leave those little flares behind your eyes
that play through shadows and faces, just like this.

Not that those shapes are ghosts, and not that
my eyes can't remember things, or tell them apart;
not that the dazzle or glitter ever falls flat;
but it glints back from however far ahead
you've gone – the hint, the something astray
and unsaid for too long, then better not said.
So we end up without a place to start,
all things being equal, with just such
disparity as the road or the weather gives
the two of us, always this far away;
or the sunlight makes you frown, in spits and spats
of rain that come to nothing, just
seeming to kiss your eyes for a second, and no more than that.

Work: 1958

Hardly another car on the whole road
to Cookstown from the far end of Tyrone;
hardly another traveller in town,
but shopkeepers and farmers by the cartload

in the Royal Hotel, piled up at a bar
so busy now, so packed, that there's barely
room to lean across, or to catch the ear
of a customer among this crowd in early

for the weekend, scarcely time to catch the eye
of a barman working himself off his feet;
matches, and just one goodwill round to buy,
then back to the lodging house in Union Street,

where scarcely a word passes, as you sit
down to a tea of half-stale soda farls
and eggs fried hard: at last a cigarette,
then your letter home, to 17, Mount Charles,

from which address, six months or more ago,
you buried your father, a private, estranged man
you hardly knew, and now will never know.
Picking up samples outside in the van,

you wonder where this leads, and where it ends:
a cold March night washed up in Cookstown;
saddlery and leather; an uncle who sends
you everywhere but home; and the road down

towards forty, blind and narrow with the grime
and smoke you breathe in, sharp as the night air –
but you know all the roads, the time served there:
the boredom and the sorrow and the time.

Foreknowledge

That nothing comes or goes at this hour,
when poems are ticking over in the dark
and everything here is the same colour,
long before dawn's handiwork
can begin to show or tell
or count for much, if it will count at all.

Maybe then, with plenty to admire,
– the room assembling itself, her face
familiar again, as the same face –
the day will come in, brisk and spruce,
sure of itself, with energy to spare
and time to burn. This hurts; it will hurt more.

The Victory Weekend

May 1945/ May 1995

Friday

At six, we went to drink beer on the roof:
  we hoisted ourselves up the dusty steps
that gave straight on to slates, and sat aloof
  from London, with its parapets and rooftops

stretching away in straight lines everywhere,
  on level terms now with the moving trees
that stood together hugely in the square,
  then balanced tumblers gently on our knees

so that, while all around us still there rose
  the last of Friday's heat, now we would pass
a half-hour until dusk in hunched repose,
  cold light between our fingers and cold glass

like talismans, or prizes lately won,
  tokens of lead and water turned to gold
and turned to catch the sun, full of the sun;
  their wink and glint ours now to have and hold.

The glasses empty, we edged back again
  to switch on lights, and change, then wander down
to streets that were still warm, with lane on lane
  of buses and hot cars all set for town

but nudging forward only by degrees,
  while we half-ran ahead, still hand in hand,
keeping our balance with a certain ease,
  or flying, really, not needing to land;

we leaned into each other as we turned
  tight corners of short cuts, and rattled past
tourists in lines, the beggars that they spurned
  and we left standing, getting there at last

a minute or two early, out of breath,
    then up more staircases, against the odds
to beat the curtain and perch just beneath
    the high roof on our cheap seats in the gods.

That night King Arthur and his Britons made
    their stand against the entire Saxon race,
Woden and all those other gods of the shade
    who hid in woods and caves, in every dark place,

a standing army of warlocks, spirits, nymphs
    emerging naked from enchanted streams
where they might tempt the hero with a glimpse
    of breasts in half-light, haunt him down in dreams,

then drag him to his ruin in the mere;
    the forest trees were something more than trees:
one nick, and they might cry aloud for fear
    or anguish, one false note and they would seize

a man and send him reeling through the air;
    while music zoomed and buzzed and sang up high
bad spirits and good, that flitted everywhere,
    parleyed and fought across a painted sky.

After his unsurprising victory
    brought the land back to Arthur mile by mile,
from cliffs far over the delighted sea
    out came at last the Spirit of the Isle

who sang to Purcell's music Dryden's words,
    a rising measure for the planets above,
and swept on inland, to the flocks and herds
    at peace in the seat of pleasure and of love,

in time with pastoral, a new-blooded nation
    ready to stretch now into its great year
with harmony and thunder, jubilation,
    and minds serene and calm and free from fear.

We left there, jittery with spectacle
    and full of music, at the music's speed;
London transfigured, half a miracle,
    but half something expected, took the lead

and steered us both, in giddy loops, zig-zags,
    to the flat, to bed, and through the panoply
of streets packed out with foreigners and flags
    in a city all dressed up for victory.

Saturday

Wellington, Blenheim, Spitfire, Hurricane:
    the name for each familiar silhouette,
labouring like a model aeroplane
    up there in thin formation, was pre-set

in what I learned, like most boys of my age,
    from war-comics, from films on TV,
when fighting men would slash the screen and page
    with blinding fire, or screams of agony –

exotic cries from Germans or Japanese
    at the extremities of pain and fear
were more grist to the mill: we took up these
    in playgrounds where the War went on all year,

when stockpiled arms were both elaborate
    and fiercely imagined, every shell
had its right calibre, all accurate
    as little pedants moved in for the kill.

Knowing their names, I pored over the sky,
    and as the planes kept up their stately pace
I stood in close to you, watching them fly
    over us and away, until no trace

was left in clouds or the resounding air
    of shapes familiar fifty years ago,
engines once listened out for everywhere,
    a drum and buzz distinct from the known, low

thrumming of German bombers on the nights
    when London took a pasting and took fire,
cascades of bombs setting its heart alight
    to leave it by daytime a smouldering pyre

with figures like stick-figures in attendance
    – fire hoses and tin helmets, stretcher-men
to bear away the dead with routine patience,
    black tons of rubble, miles of rot and ruin –

then life resuming stubbornly all around
    with boredom and endurance hedging bets
on who would win the day, and the days drowned
    in weak beer, wrapped in smoke from cigarettes.

When I was born, the whole show had been over
    for seventeen years; a new and stilted war
was being played behind-hand, under cover,
    with solid counters ready everywhere:

Castro and Kennedy, the Bay of Pigs;
    Berlin smashed and possessed and cut in two:
prowled over by B-52s and MIGs,
    Europe was scarcely likely to pull through,

so the last War went into storybooks,
    and boys pretending to be soldiers crept
up on each other, while jumpily in nooks
    and crannies all the stealthy missiles slept

their way through a strange peacetime, and through whole
    decades of stand-off, bluff, and false alarm,
as I slogged out the long campaign through school
    and won it, having come to no real harm.

Now you and I watched ribbons dip and swag
    where fast jets smashed and screamed over the Mall,
spreading the colours of the Union Flag
    behind them in a single billowy trail

that seemed to be taken up all through the crowd –
    those hats and t-shirts in red, white, and blue,
the streamers and the shell-suits, those pale, proud
    faces of a belated, happy few

in thousands upon thousands, in one place,
    as if the War was ending for the first time
here and today, as if the closest race
    was won, and peace was novel and sublime

as food or beer or sunshine or deep sleep
    to men starved and exhausted and worked dumb
who know for now the prize is theirs to keep,
    the day of execution will not come.

All fantasy: their fantasies; my own;
    the show an exercise in make-believe
disguised as memory; all the overblown
    music and glitter of a coarse, naive

history-carnival with its royalty
    and TV cameras, but no catch of pain;
cheap victory; boozy fellowship; a free
    people forgetting everything again

in a rush, as flags wave and the songs are sung
    just like before, but nothing like before:
something was wrong, or I was in the wrong
    place, but I needed to hear and see no more,

I don't know why. That day, we walked for miles
    out through the celebrations and away
to an empty City, the Barbican, St Giles
    dwarfed there in Cripplegate, its stones awry

and built over with brick, since the bombs burst
    everything open, scattering the bones
of Milton and John Foxe with fire and tempest
    where now only the blind sunlight bore down.

We walked up Moorgate then to Bunhill Fields,
    alone with a hundred thousand of the dead
jumbled beneath our feet, where old ground yields
    nothing – not an inch – to the heaviest tread,

the same hard earth where, packed away, the crazed
    bones of William Blake are lying deep
and sightless in oblivion, unraised
    for ever in unmarked and boundless sleep,

so steady they were not shaken by the bombs
    those years ago, so set and straitly laid
that they will be secure, whatever comes
    to blast or blitz the city where they hide

in the long nonsense of futurity
    when memory will forget itself, let go,
and leave the dead to their conspiracy
    of quietness, mute echo, afterglow.

Tired out, we dawdled back towards the crowds
    on holiday, like us, while the May sun
cast from behind a pinkish stream of clouds
    its sharp, indifferent light on everyone.

Sunday

The narrow and wide streets were trodden grass
    between marquees and stages in Hyde Park
as you and I edged slowly through the mass
    of trippers who had chosen to embark,

like us, for the improvised and busy town
    islanded here in green, where stalls and tents
stood in straight ranks, good servants of the Crown,
    for veterans in their different regiments

who gathered like so many new recruits,
    waiting for something – for unlikely showers,
with their umbrellas, blazers and lounge-suits
    slightly too large; for tea at all hours,

or for a known face to approach and speak
     in a familiar language some good word
to make sense in the hubbub, however weak
     that voice, or however poorly it was heard.

Their Sunday glances searched and drew a blank,
     for we were on our way home, by midday,
and hurried on, giving neither name nor rank,
     against the crowd's flow, two specks in its way,

to find ourselves on time for the train back
     to Bristol, riding westward on our own
(or nearly) down the miles of Brunel's track
     away from the weekend, away from London,

and landed before long in our attic space
     that looked straight into clouds over the Downs,
where we and the great elms sat face to face
     with ringdoves, finches, rooks in their black gowns,

where a purlin squeaked and scraked in gusts of wind
     and rooftiles thrummed through days and nights of rain,
but where now only thin shadows inclined
     across the carpet, as every windowpane

fielded a sky full of the sun, a glare
     in which the birds were tiny shadows, strafed
with light, while through that blanket fire the blare
     of high coarse voices as they chased and chafed

– seagulls in raiding-parties from the coast –
     haunted the air, became the daylight's sound,
but an all-clear too, a sign we had not lost,
     sharp and intact, re-echoing all around.

Wrapped up in peace, I was nearly twelve years old,
     waiting for school to finish for the day:
rain in the light, the weather turning cold,
     traffic outside with traffic in its way

not moving, locked on the Stranmillis Road,
    on the Malone and Lisburn Roads, stacked down
to Shaftesbury Square, or where some episode
    or other must have closed the heart of town,

and taking it for granted, thinking past
    diversions and stopped buses, through road-blocks
and windows strapped with tape against the blast
    of bombs not yet exploded, or the shocks

that glass was heir to; I would sit and wait
    for twenty to four, the bell, and day-release,
the slow trek across town to be home late,
    through desolation with the name of peace,

a burst map of the past, claims and admissions,
    abstracted history cracked up, falling in
with the blown brick and concrete, dull attritions
    of a war I didn't start and couldn't win.

The burn of sunset now, two decades on,
    lit miles of sky in coral and louder red:
I was safe; the past was over; the sun shone
    pitilessly on me and all the dead,

for this was pastoral; I could almost see
    the dead together in a wall of light,
closing their hearts, climbing away from me,
    into a ghost-glare early in the night,

in march-past, in a simple, strict parade,
    until the fireworks split up in the dark,
each flash and blur, each crack and sudden fade
    of colour an after-image, a faint mark

coming and going in the uncurtained room
    where we both sat it out, up in the air,
in the rush and rustle, click and smack and boom
    of lights as they sprayed and scattered everywhere.

Least Harm

Enough just to be there,
taken right down, apart
to the frame just, the skeleton,
barely there,
enough to say it enough of that
whatever else again,
but there just, whatever
good it is or it does.

A History Channel

If I watch any more, I'll start to be seen
mostly in black and white, coming and going
in silence, moving too fast, and when I do speak,
speaking continually in a clipped accent;
the friends who recognise me on the screen
where I train binoculars on a white Atlantic
will soon get used to this, to when I'm showing,
and when not to listen to those level, bleak
sentences all about taking it, and going to it,
in an archive voice, brassy with death and the distance.

Stick-figures move a little on the deck
of a corvette sailing placidly away
to join the convoy that will never come back,
and I do what I can to provide a soundtrack
for this or any other last appearance –
You are my sunshine, the pulse of a big band,
and the possibility that skies are grey
is all beyond me, utterly beyond
the vanishing men who vanished long since
in boats and slow freighters into an actual silence.

But it all has to be jaunty and remote
as stagy Greeks, with their archaic manners,
inclining over spears or cigarettes
while they stream forever down the busy channel,
just specks in radar, to flare one by one
in reddened smoke or the cold bitter water;
the shapes you make out are their silhouettes,
black figures walking at you from the sun,
speechless while the programme speaks by rote
in someone's voice: how this is it, and how they go to it.

The Resurrection of the Soldiers

Stanley Spencer

Of course the walls are silent, but
can music be implicit there?
What horns and pumping trumpets, shut
in paint, might blast and shake the air?

What happens when the skies unclose,
and how does the sour ground come fresh?
How freely do the worms compose
their variations on the flesh?

Two Memorials at Gilnahirk

1

He was stuck fast, I suppose, in his twenties,
the soldier who was never to be
my grandfather, who left home for the War
and who died there soon,

obediently, like others, and unremarkably;
who left his wife, and left a pair of sons,
and whose young ghost, as it leaned on the half-door,
watched lives not his fold up and unfold:

my grandmother, with hard years in front of her,
the Dromore man she married, and the hearth cold
when he died, early too; the new children;

his wife then, going blind as she grew old,
more of a stranger to him, with the names of everyone
a muddle; a straight and handsome widow woman.

2

Details that mattered, and still matter, are gone,
and the best I can do with them is pilfer
bits and pieces, for I can't be sure
exactly what it is I'm building on

as I balance and prop and jam together
parts for this rickety memorial:
the soldier's name must have been Moore,
but his Christian name? And my grandfather,

was it Dromara he came from, not Dromore?
I lean invisibly on a boundary wall
to watch over my mother in the next war,

as she reaches to take her brother Sidney's hand
on the Rocky Road, where her brothers Charlie and James,
and even the dog Major, all answer to their names.

Spillage

Night after night, my stare fixed itself on the dark
as if to stare it down – as if – as if to see
form a circle of light would help light break
and leak from the edges into my eyes, insidiously,
like days and days of rain, then pools of rainwater
ready to seep and spill in a wash, a slow flood
of splattery colours that might dry out now, or later,
or never dry in the wet recesses they had filled:

a sky so parched and papery, so low and far
stretched I couldn't see around it, or see past it
(as if wet eyes, sore words or feelings could get past it),
when daylight, broad or rainy, or just dull,
outlasts all this – all that – keeps and dissolves it all
in a standstill: for not a day passes, not an hour.

Words for a Poem

The piece of paper (one piece of paper) these words are written on
   is already in tatters, pulled to pieces and scrunched
up to litter a room – and it's *your* room, in this instance –
   where someone is crying, and someone is silent with rage.
Whatever is up in the air, the air is crackly and bitter,
   unbreatheable, the bits of paper are breaths
ripped away, but they won't go away; at this moment
   tears are all over your eyes, you can't see a stime,
but this page can tell you he's there still, with a face on him
   like a man who has bitten on a clove, or drunk eisel.

The Cloud

Near the beginning, it must be a summer's day,
we are together in a black-and-white garden
in front of the greenhouse, you on your knees
and me with my hands on my knees, our faces level,
and smiling into the sunlight for the camera.
We both look shy there, even of each other,
as we wait to hear the shutter clunk, to get up
and out of the glare, then move further apart
as you go inside to practise the piano
and I am driven home, where I forget all this.

I must be two years old in the photograph
and you are maybe fourteen; can you tell me?
The last time I saw you, I was too shy to speak:
but you are a girl still, and I am a man,
muddled and sour and a grown man
with things to tell you, which you will never hear
as my voice loses its way between us.
Face to face, I touch your cheek with a finger,
and where I breathe now on your smile
a cloud comes. It would take the light from your eyes.

August

I was trying to read, but the terrible lights and splatter
of rain wild on the gutters and tiles, on the back window,
were too much; I touched off the lamp and just watched
houses and trees light up and go dark, then light up again –

nobody out but one couple drenched through, arm in arm,
running; thunder building and collapsing at intervals
like bombs going off across town; and me closed
in the roof, in my crow's nest or eyrie, if that's what it is.

At Rosses Point

The map in my hands is done,
so I walk here in niggling rain
away past the road, its forgotten
corners and slow bends,
its loops and drops and its dead-ends,
until the only thing that's plain
around each curve of the level shore
is somebody – you, then you again –
waiting incredibly for me there.

I might as well be the metal man
who moves not an inch in years
with the sea around him, a lamp in his hands,
as touch your lips or your hair
while your body is vanishing everywhere,
flesh that appears and disappears
in places like this, where light dispels
or conjures it, as the map of my palm
opens and closes on shells, the actual shells.

Travellers

Last night I dreamed he came back from the dead,
wearing the slate-black overcoat I wore
to his Christmas funeral; and what we said
to calm each other shook us all the more,
fragile with love, that old embarrassment,
no secret, or a secret badly kept,
that burst out into pure astonishment
and weeping in the end, for we both wept.

I saw him see me as he saw me last,
with pleasantries and little else to say
(as often, and as usual, in the past),
a formal man, now middle-aged and tall,
in travelling clothes, ready to go away,
when I held and kissed him in the hospital.

The Long Look

On a scooped-out wall, far underground,
after centuries of darkness and no air,
from flaky plaster, just as they were found,
the painted figures flourish and stare
at you, or at no one in particular.

You can't return their looks, or recognise
them always for the strangers that they are:
in fancy dress, and with slow upturned eyes,
all of them seem to be intent elsewhere,
caught up in a distance that is far too far.

But stranger that you are, you see something,
and carry something back up to the light
where vines and flowers, and real birds on the wing
jostle and clutter the edges of your sight
looking sidelong, and different, and not right.

The Road to Rome

Dust in the umbrella pines
that stand and stretch in their gapped lines
on each side of the road sifts in
to colour everything; the din
of snarling Fiats on the stones
below, and the engines' gasps and groans
stop-starting at their different speeds
trouble the sparse grass and the weeds
a little, but they trouble us
more nearly now we leave the bus
and lean as far as we can lean
into the tiny verge between
the headlong cars and a steep ditch,
with noise and heat at such a pitch
that even the road to Hell today
seems safer than the Appian Way.
(At this point, from an antique past,
into my ear in broad Belfast
an unstill voice insists that I
am taking comfort in a lie,
and those two places aren't distinct
but bloodily and always linked.)
I'm otherwise determined though,
for I have to jump, at the word go,
across the cars on their rough ride
and dare myself to the other side,
arriving, as I knew I must,
already caked in sweat and dust.

To come to Rome in August is
an act of some foolhardiness
for those of us unused to heat:
yet here I am, with pounding feet
and a burnt neck, in spite of all
intent on keeping up my crawl
from site to site in morning sun,
then back indoors by the afternoon.
This morning, though it's barely ten,
is one on which more prudent men
would keep to cafés and galleries

and not set out on paths like these
from a roaring road across parched fields
where no tree, however modest, yields
so much as a scrawny shade, until
the track leads up a gentle hill
and issues in an entrance-gate
where guides and other tourists wait
in batches to go underground.

Today I'm to be shown around
by an already priestly youth,
beaming and bursting with the truth,
who comes from India; he leads
a dozen of us, some with beads
to pray by in the better rooms
among the sunken catacombs,
and burbles happily all the while
as he shepherds us, with a sure smile,
down rough steps, over bumpy floors,
into those dull red corridors
that wind and branch and ramify
for miles into the dark, where I
can all too easily begin
to visualise myself, locked in,
a wandering unquiet ghost
lost, and imprisoned with the lost
along the remoter galleries.
For all the snappy homilies
he makes at every turn and twist,
the gloom here helps me to resist
our guide's too zealous overview;
for the sad truths are hardly new:
against death's evidence everywhere
his voice's frail career in air
is something infinitely small,
a single, echoless footfall
where silence takes in everything.
What meagre history I can bring
down with me to these deathly streets
restates, reiterates, repeats
over and over the single rule
taught in its hard and tedious school,
how memory and firm belief

obliged at last to come to grief
perpetuate an old design,
and always need to blur the line
between dumb hope and vanity.
Down passages I scarcely see
the dead ranged once on either side,
but not without some measured pride
in family or faith; they left
tokens behind for the bereft
where rank and virtue could find mention,
as well as for God's best attention,
or for the notice of other gods –
a change of faith made little odds
to the modest or the extravagant
memorials with whose aid they went
out of the buzzing world: one wall
keeps delicate portraits a foot tall,
where, framed by intricate designs
of peacocks, flowers and heavy vines,
intent upon some heavenly crown,
the dear departed stare us down
whose eyes, looking away, look through
us and our own contingent view.

The Indian novice's upbeat
and chatty commentary makes neat
distinctions where things should be blurred:
here, Christ about to give the word
for Lazarus to come, is less
himself than he is Orpheus,
and, working miracles with ease,
shades elsewhere into Hercules.
Despite the martyrs stacked around,
this ground is also pagan ground,
and several tombs on their long lets
seem cannily to be hedging bets
between two worlds at subtle strife
on tickets for the future life.
When some of the better families
moved out from their good premises
in the city, they found here instead
a swish suburbia of the dead
and later, as more Christians came

to swell the ranks, these were the same
addresses that kept up their price
and added features to entice
the faithful here, with martyrs and
late popes in popular demand
(good company for when the skies
roll open, and the bodies rise),
until the district grew at last
a crowded place, with deep and vast
recesses and branching avenues
of the shelved dead in stacks and queues
patiently waiting for the end.
Now, as our chipper Indian friend
lights up the dreary neighbourhood
with the force of his 'the martyrs' blood!',
I'd like to hear the ghosts agree
as they turn in their sleep, and we
leave them secure in stone and clay
to snuggle up till Judgement Day
when Hell and Heaven, black and white,
utter darkness, utter light,
split in an instant, and for ever.

For now, the more mundane endeavour
to keep our footing on the stairs
absorbs us all, as our way bears
narrowly up and sharp around
to the blasting daylight above ground.
As the guide's parting pieties
speed us out on our day-release
I find some shade and, book in hand,
replot the daring route I'd planned
to bring me home, but sense the heat
still rising, and opt to retreat
to *via Appia* and the bus.
Forgetting my gloomy-ponderous
pontifications in the dark,
I'm more than ready to embark
on the road to Rome, and lunch, and soon
siesta through the afternoon.

(At odds with so much here, I want
to air my bumptious, Protestant

certainties and predispositions
– just call them foregone intuitions –
and, fresh from the stale catacomb,
confess myself dyed in the womb
in colours now indelible
I wouldn't want to change at all.
It's ten years on since first I came
to visit Rome, and still the same
gripes and frustrations and ill-will
mingle with every simpler thrill
in plenty here; though deep in thrall
to the peculiar pastoral
(part history and part escape),
I'm haunted often by the shape
of an old enemy on the stones:
the disapproval in my bones
for all the bulging pomp remains
distinct as ever, and maintains
its staunch dissenting line, while I
saunter beneath a Roman sky
and, hammered by the sunshine, lurch
from church to gilded baroque church,
admiring and deploring on
like some off-duty puritan,
delighted and appalled to find
himself so little colourblind.)

The sun high up gets stronger by
the minute, and the minutes fly;
the time for me to set my face
towards a journey home, and pace
myself along the burning track
is more than come; I stagger back,
casting no shadow on the white
path where among the stones a bright
and tiny lizard, green and blue,
has scamper-scuttled into view
for half a second, and is gone
as quickly; pushing on and on,
I trample pale and scalding coals
and come to where the traffic rolls
downhill to Rome; again I make
the leap of faith that is the break-

neck crossing, and I live to see
the further side, and sanctuary:
small houses closed against the heat;
the travellers who stand and wait;
thin fences strung with wire and rust,
and pines the colour of the dust.

An Alarm

At dawn, the gulls call out to one another
and crowd the bedroom with their gawky cries,
so that we waken, as if to a child's cries,
all summer early, with nothing like surprise.

The Blood-Bruise

I worked against it all that afternoon,
the racing bindweed, or convolvulus,
that had gone unchecked, it seemed, by anyone
for weeks, and now made its calamitous
faces everywhere: those deathly-delicate
trompettes, and their lime-white
mouths that opened up, and opened again,
in silent and proliferating forms
strung along cords I had to bundle down
and gather up as tangles in my arms.

I stooped in to the stricken rosebushes
where they had all but given up the ghost
so deeply had the bindweed's ropes and lashes
become involved, and so nearly had they lost
the plot to its inveigling flowers and leaves;
as thorns plucked at my sleeves
I hauled in slippery tendrils by the yard
until my arms could hold no more, my arms
that, now I looked, had been scrabbed and scarred
where they and the sharp roses came to terms.

What I saw then, when I saw you suddenly,
knocked me off-kilter, like a freak shot
or a punch from nowhere, making light of me:
it wasn't even your face at first, and not
your blue-green eyes as they took in my alarm,
but the blood-bruise on your arm
where the skin was softest; where, as I looked,
I almost tracked the course a vein might run
minutely under my fingers; where they unhooked
and undid you, when all of their work was done.

Standstill

There is a house where all the doors are closed:
I can see this house from the outside in,
and they watch me, looking from the inside out
at a morning, a particular one in the autumn,
with somebody there just standing under the trees
who can look in and see them still looking
back at him, wondering when he will come,
as he asks himself why he left, and when he did,
why each step forwards is a step further away
from a house with all the windows and the doors closed.

A Fall

I wake up from a dream about being in America
to a blackbird holding its own against the early traffic;
in the dream, I was jumping on solid ground
to prove that it was there, as the blackbird also proves itself
in a bleary dawn, where now fog proves that it is autumn.

The Conversion

Then in September came the plague of spiders.
How many tens or dozens
in the one week might have slipped inside
and set up shop with threads and muslins
strung out from the corners, I could hardly tell;
but they found me everywhere, at all hours,
as they raced down walls, or hared along the floors,
tumbling, or sticking at a point, deathly still.

So the spiders took possession of my house
and I, convinced they were unlucky to kill,
left them to their businesses in autumn rooms
and closed the doors
to settle, touchily, in a dark place
and coddle in my hands a pint of gall.

The Risk

The chances are this won't work:
taking in swatches of early light
(half-light, either early or late)
these sore eyes tell me I'm awake

and now, whatever the chances are,
the game and I no longer match,
for I can't win, or win much,
with losses harder and harder to bear –

downturns, upsets, all-out collapse,
a dead-end at the end of luck
where I might stick, or might be stuck,
waiting for sudden breaks and slips

in the brilliant game being played through
before my eyes, its risk of loss
as nothing to this need to lose
it all now on one losing throw.

The Mild Autumn

I'm back, and the mild autumn is here too,
where by this time in October usually
the trees are stripped down, and a flooding wind
has come with sleet and cold, to stay for good.

But this year we are having a mild autumn,
and I am home to see you in October
when every day the sun keeps flooding
into these rooms where, for a while, I'll stay

and where, for a while, we have each other back,
so that today I needn't watch my time
as we wait, not saying much, and half shut down,
for the pools results or the next meal to come.

With the winter holding back for good, we both
suppose that this might usually be the way,
that the winds will keep down, and the cold
evenings and days will not come, after all;

suppose I may stay here, or might never have gone,
where the trees with all their leaves in flood
are never stripped, and where the night comes down
without a breath of cold when it comes to stay.

Two Spiders

The first has been dead for a long time
– and this is, in any case, a long time ago –
when it falls, or it drops, or slow-slides
out of a book I've opened and won't read
(in the bedroom, in the sunlight, in an odd moment)
next to weightless in my palm.
This is a black spider, and the book
has a dedication in copperplate French
where the dark ink has faded and blurred slightly,
to whom, and from whom, I don't know.

The other spider suddenly came to light
as I leaned and caught a sleeve in the hedge,
and it fiddles with my shirt-cuff for dear life now
over a precipice, till I cup it in a palm
where it is waiting, or I make it wait,
for one thing or the other. It's a blurry white
against the colour I am, or my hand is,
like a letter fading out or fading in from somewhere
that might belong to any standard message
sent from the dead to the dead, for no reason.

Hush

Speak these words, in this order, pause
where rest is called for; it will not be my voice
you hear, or sound like mine: there is no choice
but to accept this, and no other cause
to plead against pure silence at the end
except to say (and softly, slowly say)
that nothing will replace the sounds today
the hedges make here, as they give and bend
with the invisible mild breeze
that comes from nowhere, simmering and seething
up through acres of fields and miles of trees
until it reaches this blind place, like grief,
like one long sob without change or relief;
but it's not that. When I breathe, it's not me breathing.

Leopardi

Seashells

As I look now, you are starting to look through me,
out as far as wherever the tide has gone,
while clouds bundle sunlight from Inishowen
over our heads, and our slow walk, rained-on,
into a windy glare of salt and ozone
is something very gradually lost to view.

These empty shells are brittle as your bones,
and here's one with a thread of amber-brown
that runs around then runs out in a spiral
into my palm. Now I am the colour of sand
on soft ground paved with only shells
for your hazel eyes, that are starting to cloud over.

The Full House

For decades, when you think of Union Street,
you mention how one night the house was crammed
so tightly men lay on the stairs and landing,
– travellers in this and that, from all parts –
one slumped half-upright by a corner wall,
one wedged under a table; and all but you
are sleeping there, packed in and packed away:
motionless all the night, they never waken.

Work: 1998

These buildings are heartbroken for the city –
it failed them, and they failed it, long ago;
even dignity has been saved too long here,
and it turns bad in a faint tide of spring air
where I must walk more than a mile uphill,
past the same places to work every day:
the places hurt me now; maybe we hurt each other.

Time wastes the stone. Some quarrels are past mending:
the word is attrition, a sure wearing-down,
pointless and relentless like the weather;
meetings are a circus of self-regard,
a freakshow, where the dwarf and the lion-lady
are trapped in themselves, and stuck with each other
for good, and where I too am a fixture.

Everyone fails: my heart works overtime,
pumping round venom and gall; it wears down
all concerned, till the rooms stink of exhaustion.
Time drains into the stone, and drains away
like the sweat of slaves, while I learn the tricks
and turns of a performer, trained to do
business with the implacable and the mad.

At night, I half-run downhill to the station,
past places that can tear me up in ribbons
and mean to; my heart stalls and starts again,
and it all goes through me like a lifting wave,
transparent, if not clear; treading a void,
I watch my steps leading me everywhere
on a fast road, deliberate and faithless.

The Stand-Off

To say anything now is to risk it all:
and both of them know how it is all risk
at this proximity; how it's somebody's call,
as they stare each other out like basilisk
and gorgon; how it's someone's turn to break
rank, even a rank of one, for form's sake.

Perhaps they were lovers once, or may become so –
it doesn't matter: what they say in the end
will be formal and inscrutable, for show,
full of what has been and what might be said,
and in no language that can give or bend.

Ready to take each other to their knees,
they stand on motionless by the made bed
with faces set, guests of the thief Procrustes.

The Thread

How slightly, twenty years ago,
I managed to construe the girl
I met three times, or twice, then so
awkwardly flirted with, by proxy,
dispatching printed poems of mine
whose frail and thin-spun lines
took scarcely any weight (I see
that much), carried no weight at all.

In a bored moment, by sheer chance,
news of her death crosses my eyes,
and minutes pass while I realise
that now, at this far distance,
I can't so much as picture her,
feeling for the least snag or pull
in a line that's barely visible,
and slighter than a thread of hair.

Damon the Mower

The beer in my fist is a bar of gold, and bitter;
the taste in my mouth is only the taste of cold.
I watch the punters, and see people who aren't here,
catching in a girl's drunk laugh another's shriek–sob
as she tells and blurts and gasps out what has to be told:

how some yob in a suit thinks he thinks the whole world of her;
how he dresses her up in shoes and stockings and lace and gold;
how he loves her so much, he took the blunt stub of a glass and
                                                             hit her;
how I'm her last and only hope, her one true friend:
how it's come to an end, though it's always coming to an end.

I'm tasting again the salt-bitter tears on her cheek
as I drink down shots of alum, vinegar, eisel, gall,
to take the first and only dope, this mild and meek
fall-guy down for a fall, a taste of blood and bruises,
like a man who asks *What is it?* and knows rightly what it is.

The Way to Lose

Tonight again I thought I could see your face crying,
but in a mirror, and only reversed, dry tears
coated my cheeks and my lips, as I watched the lying
words come out backwards: this for months; for years.

Fireworks

in memory of Sheila Smyth

1

As I walked to the appointment with you at my heels,
I could hear my own steps fall on the pavement
and was thankful for the gravity of new shoes
with their sounding weight against the clean-washed stone.
I thought I might be leaving a trail of sparks,
but knew if I looked round there would be only
daylight, no glimmer-glitz, and no glamour
of faceted and soon-gone lightning; no,
not you even, whom I'd just asked along
to lend what weight you could to the proceedings,
and keep up with me for these last few paces.

2

It was like putting a match
to a tablet, or a lozenge,
then starting to watch
this dot with a fizz and fringe
of tiny sparks flare up
in the blacked-out sitting-room:
above the saucer a beam,
a pillar of deep light
that would rasp, change colour, then drop,
at its prime some five or six
inches tall, if that.

We had bought indoor fireworks:
in half an hour, an entire box
had been set up, set off,
and burned away (no match
for the real thing, and no
real thing that year anyhow).
They didn't come to much,
but I said I liked them, half
to please people, half
to reassure myself; and now,
in daylight, look: a room
where the dead sit down with strangers
after tea at Hallowe'en;
laid out in the middle of this
are fireworks like sweeties –
jelly beans, pastilles, and cinnamon
lozenges (properly, *lozengers*).

3

I was going somewhere fast, or seemed to be:
I remember the hurry, the blind panics and flare-ups,
me lying awake all night in Dunluce Avenue
hearing everything in the world that ever moved;
but up in the air mostly, with the illusion of speed,
and the conviction that I must be weightless.
While the ground beneath me seemed to vanish,
you knew what to say and what not to say.

I did nothing – stuck, weighed down, engrossed even –
after our friend had told me you were dying:
the right or the wrong words wouldn't have mattered,
and what I took for speed was just things moving
in one direction all the time, with me
slow to make ground: too slow, if anything.

Eclogue

It's as though the fields around these parts
had been written over as well as worked
for generations: cuneiform straws
tumble and stick across the ground
for me and a few sorry birds
to worry over, as the day ends
in bluster and half-hearted rain.
A car drips quietly in the lay-by,
unlocked, and with the engine warm,
as I get ready to return,
picking a way through the ditch-side
scatter of votive offerings –
bottles, chip-papers, crunched-up cans
of *Harp* lager – and I keep one eye
on the familiar glare and steam-boil
of clouds and sun on this horizon
changing the weather over and over.
This time tomorrow, I'll be gone
– or back to where I'm gone from now –
and the light and drizzle, the baffling wind
that come and go on the Castlereagh hills
all morning and all afternoon
will come and go again, without me.

Come on – for you know rightly now
it's time for you to be away:
in an hour or two, the shuttle flight
will put your head back in the clouds,
heaving you up over the shipyard
and out across the water again.
In your mind's eye, you see this place
from the air mostly, reduced to shapes,
clouds and cloud-shadows, farms, towns,
always becoming smaller and more
blurred in the melancholy distance.
Down here, things sharpen and mean less:
it's not the best place, not the worst.

I envy you the grip and focus
on everything I can't possess:
I'm lost to home, as home is lost

to me, and there's no going back –
just visiting and visiting,
where my mind puts a shadow down
across the landscape, drained away
into near-perpetual dusk.

What happens here is real, mundane:
dusk only comes at daylight-fall,
and lives get led without you here.
You look at the high Braniel road
and see it thirty years ago:
I wasn't born then, and the whole
bad-time history leaves me cold.
You're hypnotised by the stupid past,
and just because you can't get loose
from its clutches, you expect to preen
your feathers while you lick your wounds,
then turn the lot into dismay
and sadness that seeps everywhere
in the end, doomy, absolute.
If you knew it, there's a future too –
not glamorous, maybe, but it's there;
and every detail of the day
can scarcely answer to the gloom
you always want to paint across it:
there's money here, and the normal mix
of family, routine, good times;
no need for me to shrink or cringe,
for I'm secure with what I am
and don't need to apologise.
Isn't that better? And the truth is
there's peace now – peace: you can hardly
bring yourself to say the word.

I'm never at peace, for it's one thing
or another that distresses me,
distracts me, through the day and half
the night; but most of all, simply
these hills and roads, the people here,
or here no longer, the thin ghosts:
I keep on looking out for them
or listening for their voices in mine.
One summer night, on the walk up

from the Knock Road to Mann's Corner,
Charlie Moore saw the crooked back
and shoulders, and the bowed-down head
of an old farmer, sitting still
on a wall, who had worked the land
a century before; the Rocky Road
at Gilnahirk, still overgrown
when I was young, a boundary
between our steps and the graveyard,
keeps watch over the newly dead
and my own father now, a guest there.
To see peace, and peace only, is
to see the living and not the rest,
as though to shade your eyes in sun
and pick your way through grassy ruins,
scarcely able to look up.
That's why the light and shadows here
transfix me, why some future is
an abstract blur against the sharp
presence of figures in this landscape.
Nothing is new, and it can't be:
liars who talk about history
as something whose warm hand they feel
guiding them in a chosen path
vanish, and never answer to
all of the anger or the grief;
their words hide most of what they mean,
and when they smile into your face,
they don't mean words. It's time to go.
From here, the lights of Belfast look
like a huge diagram, with the city
a puzzle putting itself together
by trial and error, piece by piece,
as traffic bellows into the sky.

We'll go together on the drive,
and maybe have the time for one
more coffee in Departures; look,
the last of the sun is cutting straight
through the hedgerow, and our two
thin shadows have begun to stretch
into each other along the road.

The Company

They're not all old, and he's about my age,
this one who waddles out of his road towards me
and says what he can; I say back what I can,
then hear him breathing his way on to somewhere.

The bald man with no bowels left is searching
for his absent brother, and looks even under the beds
about this time every night; he keeps asking
the same question, and not hearing the same replies,

while a boy with plummy eyes and a mashed face
takes ten minutes to get out of his bed,
to assemble himself, his legs and his purple arms
with minutest care, and wait outside then for nothing.

Everybody gets what's coming: even the police
know this, who can set questions about bones
and bruises unknown to the doctors; missing persons
keep company with visitors in their cars

all the way home, and they stay not there
like a pain that's gone and might be coming back
when some little something
grows, and takes hold, and finds out what it's looking for.

The Proof

One birthday I came to see you out of the blue,
and walked in on you, in your usual chair,
and a flood of papers, pools-coupons and pens,
where, just for a second, you looked me through
and through, as though between us a cloudy lens
gave grounds for doubt that I was there at all.
The proof is there if you want it to be there:
once I had left my bag down in the hall
I came on in, and came back in to normal.

Our manners held, and still they hold us steady,
for although I don't appear now just for form's sake,
I seem to know the proper way to find you,
busy as ever, waiting there at home,
as if we knew the best way to make ready,
the two of us, by instinct, and by proof:
silently almost, and while I've hardly noticed,
you have made your way out of the sitting-room,
closing the door very quietly behind you.

The Back Roads

You had come so close, that when I woke
to the phone, and answered half-asleep,
there was a voice from the dead that spoke
to a sunken distance – faint, miles deep –

at a loss to figure some way back
and calling from the further bank
to the son who lost you – who lost track
of plastic boats that dipped and sank,

or a kite that crashed at the Giant's Ring,
the loop-the-loops and vanishing-tricks
of gliders, tangled yards of string,
then crumpled balsa and splintered sticks

all lost, and your voice with them lost –
but I came to, and the voice was real,
no rivers and no lines were crossed,
no boat with a crimped and crinkled sail

or aeroplane with bent-back wings
had come to grief in the water there;
as usual, we said usual things
on our back roads to everywhere.

The Watercolourists

It is six in the evening in the nineteenth century,
and I join the watercolourists on the Aventine
who are all sitting forwards in one straggly line
completely intent, and never noticing me,
as they work and watch, quickly, silently,
to catch the sky in a violet bruise or a stain
that seeps into their paper, almost weighing it down,
the distant and near colours all that they can see.

Rome is below us, where sheep still haunt the Forum,
and I know I am with the busy dead, for here
is my own great-grandfather, John Graham,
who studies the view, and paints one field in Ayrshire
for ever, utterly engrossed; in a flutter and flare
of light and water, I start work with the least of them.

Acknowledgements and Notes

Several of the poems in this book were included in the pamphlet *As if* (Thumbscrew Press, 2002). 'The poem' appeared as a limited edition publication from Cheng Press (2002).

Some poems appeared in the following publications to whose editors I am indebted: *Ambit Review*, *Temple*, *The Manse Observer*, *The Hudson Review*, *Metre*, *Poetry Ireland Review*, *PN Review*, *Thumbscrew* and *The Times Literary Supplement*. The poem 'Maud' was published in *O Vage L'Anno: at the Year's Turning* edited by Marco Sonzogni (Ordfáis Press, 1998).

I thank here especially Tim Kendall, Michael Longley and Andrew MacNeillie for their advice and support. A Fellowship at the Tyrone Guthrie Centre in 1996 is gratefully acknowledged.

The two lines of Greek in the book's epigraph are by Sappho, or out of the 2nd century AD; a literal translation is 'Echo stops and licks a tongue through the fertile meadow, answering the birds with her far-sounding voice.'

Fradubio and Fradubio in the poem 'Two Trees', are characters in Edmund Spenser's *The Faerie Queene* (Book I, Canto ii). The poem 'The Cup' translates part of the first Idyll of Theocritus; I am indebted to the edition by Richard Hunter, *Theocritus: A Selection* (Cambridge University Press, 1999). The first section of 'The Victory Weekend' draws on John Dryden's text for Henry Purcell's *King Arthur, Or, The British Worthy* (1691), and upon the performance of that opera directed by Graham Vick and conducted by William Christie at the Royal Opera House in May, 1995. 'The Solitaire' translates and adapts 'L'Infinito' by Giacomo Leopardi. 'Eclogue' imitates the first Eclogue of Virgil.